50 Farm-Fresh Milk Dishes

By: Kelly Johnson

Table of Contents

- Creamy Macaroni and Cheese
- Milk Pudding
- Homemade Ice Cream
- Milkshake
- Creamy Potato Soup
- Rice Pudding
- Milk Chocolate Fudge
- Custard
- Milk and Honey Oatmeal
- Paneer (Indian Cottage Cheese)
- Buttermilk Pancakes
- Milk Bread
- Homemade Yogurt
- Milk Biscuits
- Milk Coffee
- Creamy Alfredo Pasta
- Cheesecake
- Butter Chicken
- Milk-Based Smoothies
- Clotted Cream
- Chocolate Milk
- Milk Caramel Flan
- Dairy-Free Milk Alternatives (like Almond Milk)
- Mascarpone Cheesecake
- Panna Cotta
- Rice and Milk Soup
- Milk-Based Ice Cream Sandwiches
- Creamy Polenta
- Milk Chocolate Cake
- Sweetened Condensed Milk Cookies
- Milk-Custard Tart
- Milk Fudge (Kalakand)
- Creamy Risotto
- Churned Butter
- Hot Chocolate

- Bechamel Sauce
- Milk-Soaked French Toast
- Sweet Milk Buns
- Milk Chocolate Truffles
- Hot Milk Cake
- Milk-Based Tiramisu
- Strawberry Milk Pudding
- Milk-Cream Cheese Frosting
- Homemade Ricotta
- Sweet Milk Yogurt Parfaits
- Caramelized Milk Pudding
- Sweet Milk Tea
- Mashed Potatoes with Milk
- Milk and Banana Smoothie
- Rice Milk Chocolate

Creamy Macaroni and Cheese

Ingredients:

- 2 cups elbow macaroni
- 2 tbsp butter
- 2 tbsp all-purpose flour
- 2 cups whole milk
- 1 1/2 cups shredded sharp cheddar cheese
- 1/2 cup grated Parmesan cheese
- Salt and pepper to taste
- 1/2 tsp mustard powder (optional)
- 1/2 tsp garlic powder (optional)

Instructions:

1. Cook the macaroni according to package instructions. Drain and set aside.
2. In a large pot, melt butter over medium heat. Add flour and whisk for 1-2 minutes to form a roux.
3. Gradually pour in milk while whisking to prevent lumps. Cook for 5-7 minutes until the sauce thickens.
4. Stir in cheddar cheese, Parmesan, salt, pepper, and optional mustard or garlic powder. Stir until smooth.
5. Add the cooked macaroni to the cheese sauce and mix to coat.
6. Serve hot.

Milk Pudding

Ingredients:

- 2 cups whole milk
- 1/4 cup sugar
- 2 tbsp cornstarch
- 1 tsp vanilla extract
- A pinch of salt

Instructions:

1. In a saucepan, combine the milk, sugar, cornstarch, and salt. Stir well to dissolve the cornstarch.
2. Cook over medium heat, stirring constantly until the mixture thickens, about 5-7 minutes.
3. Remove from heat and stir in the vanilla extract.
4. Pour into serving dishes and chill for at least 2 hours before serving.
5. Serve cold, optionally with a sprinkle of cinnamon or fresh fruit on top.

Homemade Ice Cream

Ingredients:

- 2 cups heavy cream
- 1 cup whole milk
- 3/4 cup sugar
- 1 tbsp vanilla extract

Instructions:

1. In a large bowl, whisk together the cream, milk, sugar, and vanilla extract until the sugar is dissolved.
2. Pour the mixture into an ice cream maker and follow the manufacturer's instructions.
3. Once the ice cream thickens, transfer to an airtight container and freeze for at least 4 hours.
4. Scoop and serve!

Milkshake

Ingredients:

- 2 cups vanilla ice cream
- 1 cup whole milk
- 1 tsp vanilla extract (optional)
- Whipped cream (optional)

Instructions:

1. In a blender, combine ice cream, milk, and vanilla extract. Blend until smooth and creamy.
2. Pour into a tall glass and top with whipped cream, if desired.
3. Serve immediately with a straw.

Creamy Potato Soup

Ingredients:

- 4 large potatoes, peeled and diced
- 1 small onion, chopped
- 2 cloves garlic, minced
- 4 cups chicken or vegetable broth
- 1 cup whole milk
- 1/2 cup heavy cream
- 2 tbsp butter
- Salt and pepper to taste
- Chopped green onions for garnish (optional)

Instructions:

1. In a large pot, melt butter over medium heat. Add the onion and garlic, sauté until softened.
2. Add the diced potatoes and broth. Bring to a boil, then reduce heat and simmer for 15-20 minutes until the potatoes are tender.
3. Use an immersion blender to blend the soup until smooth, or transfer in batches to a regular blender.
4. Stir in the milk and heavy cream, then season with salt and pepper.
5. Heat through, and serve garnished with chopped green onions if desired.

Rice Pudding

Ingredients:

- 1 cup short-grain rice
- 4 cups whole milk
- 1/2 cup sugar
- 1 tsp vanilla extract
- 1/2 tsp ground cinnamon
- A pinch of salt

Instructions:

1. In a saucepan, combine rice, milk, sugar, cinnamon, and salt. Bring to a simmer over medium heat.
2. Reduce the heat and cook, stirring occasionally, for 25-30 minutes until the rice is tender and the pudding thickens.
3. Stir in the vanilla extract and cook for another 5 minutes.
4. Let cool slightly before serving. Serve warm or chilled, topped with additional cinnamon or fruit if desired.

Milk Chocolate Fudge

Ingredients:

- 2 cups milk chocolate chips
- 1 can (14 oz) sweetened condensed milk
- 1/4 cup unsalted butter
- 1 tsp vanilla extract
- A pinch of salt

Instructions:

1. Line an 8x8-inch baking pan with parchment paper.
2. In a saucepan, combine the chocolate chips, sweetened condensed milk, butter, and salt. Stir over low heat until the mixture is smooth.
3. Remove from heat and stir in vanilla extract.
4. Pour the mixture into the prepared pan and spread evenly.
5. Chill in the refrigerator for 2-3 hours until set.
6. Cut into squares and serve.

Custard

Ingredients:

- 2 cups whole milk
- 1/2 cup heavy cream
- 1/4 cup sugar
- 4 large egg yolks
- 1 tsp vanilla extract

Instructions:

1. In a saucepan, heat the milk and cream over medium heat until hot but not boiling.
2. In a bowl, whisk together the egg yolks and sugar until smooth.
3. Gradually whisk the hot milk mixture into the egg yolks, then return the mixture to the saucepan.
4. Cook over low heat, stirring constantly until the custard thickens and coats the back of a spoon (about 8-10 minutes).
5. Remove from heat and stir in vanilla extract.
6. Cool slightly before serving. The custard can be served warm or chilled.

Milk and Honey Oatmeal

Ingredients:

- 1 cup rolled oats
- 2 cups whole milk
- 1 tbsp honey
- 1/4 tsp cinnamon (optional)
- Pinch of salt

Instructions:

1. In a saucepan, bring milk to a simmer.
2. Add the oats, salt, and cinnamon (if using). Cook for 5-7 minutes, stirring occasionally until the oats are tender and the mixture thickens.
3. Stir in honey and cook for another minute.
4. Serve warm with additional honey or fresh fruit on top if desired.

Paneer (Indian Cottage Cheese)

Ingredients:

- 1 liter full-fat milk
- 2 tbsp lemon juice or vinegar
- A pinch of salt (optional)

Instructions:

1. Heat the milk in a heavy-bottomed pot over medium heat, stirring occasionally to prevent it from burning.
2. Once the milk comes to a boil, reduce the heat and add lemon juice or vinegar. Stir gently until the milk curdles.
3. Turn off the heat and let the milk sit for a few minutes to allow the curds to separate from the whey.
4. Line a colander with cheesecloth and pour the curdled milk through it to strain the whey.
5. Gather the cheesecloth around the curds and rinse with cold water to remove any acidity.
6. Tie the cheesecloth and hang it for 30 minutes to drain excess water.
7. Once the paneer is firm, remove it from the cloth and cut it into cubes.
8. Use it in curries, salads, or fry it as desired.

Buttermilk Pancakes

Ingredients:

- 1 cup all-purpose flour
- 1 tbsp sugar
- 1 1/2 tsp baking powder
- 1/2 tsp baking soda
- 1/4 tsp salt
- 1 cup buttermilk
- 1 egg
- 2 tbsp melted butter
- 1 tsp vanilla extract

Instructions:

1. In a bowl, mix together flour, sugar, baking powder, baking soda, and salt.
2. In a separate bowl, whisk together buttermilk, egg, melted butter, and vanilla extract.
3. Pour the wet ingredients into the dry ingredients and stir gently until combined (don't overmix).
4. Heat a non-stick skillet or griddle over medium heat and lightly grease with butter or oil.
5. Pour 1/4 cup of batter onto the skillet for each pancake. Cook until bubbles form on the surface, then flip and cook for another 1-2 minutes.
6. Serve warm with maple syrup, butter, or fresh fruit.

Milk Bread

Ingredients:

- 3 cups all-purpose flour
- 1/4 cup sugar
- 1 tsp salt
- 2 tsp active dry yeast
- 1 cup warm milk
- 2 tbsp butter, softened
- 1 egg (optional, for brushing)

Instructions:

1. In a bowl, combine warm milk and sugar. Sprinkle yeast over the milk and let it sit for 5 minutes until it becomes frothy.
2. Add flour and salt to the yeast mixture and knead to form a dough.
3. Add butter and continue kneading for 8-10 minutes until smooth and elastic.
4. Cover the dough with a damp cloth and let it rise for 1 hour or until doubled in size.
5. Preheat the oven to 350°F (175°C).
6. Punch down the dough and shape it into a loaf. Place it into a greased loaf pan.
7. (Optional) Brush the top with a beaten egg for a golden finish.
8. Bake for 25-30 minutes or until the bread is golden brown and sounds hollow when tapped.
9. Cool before slicing.

Homemade Yogurt

Ingredients:

- 1 liter whole milk
- 2 tbsp plain yogurt (with live cultures)

Instructions:

1. Heat the milk in a saucepan over medium heat, stirring occasionally until it reaches a boil.
2. Reduce the heat and simmer for 2-3 minutes. Let the milk cool to about 110°F (43°C).
3. In a small bowl, mix the yogurt with a little warm milk to create a smooth paste.
4. Stir the yogurt mixture into the warm milk.
5. Pour the milk into a clean jar or bowl, cover with a lid or cloth, and let it sit in a warm place for 6-12 hours to set.
6. Once set, refrigerate the yogurt for a few hours before serving.

Milk Biscuits

Ingredients:

- 2 cups all-purpose flour
- 2 tsp baking powder
- 1/2 tsp salt
- 1/4 cup cold butter, cubed
- 3/4 cup whole milk

Instructions:

1. Preheat the oven to 425°F (220°C).
2. In a bowl, mix flour, baking powder, and salt.
3. Add the cold butter and use a pastry cutter or your fingers to blend it into the flour mixture until it resembles coarse crumbs.
4. Gradually add the milk and stir to form a dough.
5. Turn the dough onto a lightly floured surface and knead gently for 1-2 minutes.
6. Roll the dough to 1-inch thickness and cut out biscuits using a round cutter.
7. Place the biscuits on a baking sheet and bake for 10-12 minutes or until golden brown.

Milk Coffee

Ingredients:

- 1 cup strong brewed coffee
- 1/4 cup milk
- 1 tsp sugar (optional)

Instructions:

1. Brew a strong cup of coffee using your preferred method.
2. Heat the milk in a saucepan or microwave until hot, but not boiling.
3. Pour the brewed coffee into a mug and add sugar if desired.
4. Stir in the heated milk.
5. Serve warm and enjoy!

Creamy Alfredo Pasta

Ingredients:

- 8 oz fettuccine pasta
- 1/2 cup butter
- 1 cup heavy cream
- 1 1/2 cups grated Parmesan cheese
- 2 cloves garlic, minced
- Salt and pepper to taste
- Fresh parsley, chopped (optional)

Instructions:

1. Cook the fettuccine pasta according to package instructions. Drain and set aside.
2. In a large skillet, melt butter over medium heat. Add garlic and cook for 1 minute until fragrant.
3. Add the cream and bring to a simmer. Stir in the Parmesan cheese and cook until the sauce thickens.
4. Season with salt and pepper to taste.
5. Add the cooked pasta to the skillet and toss to coat with the sauce.
6. Garnish with parsley and serve immediately.

Cheesecake

Ingredients:

- 1 1/2 cups graham cracker crumbs
- 1/4 cup sugar
- 1/2 cup melted butter
- 3 packages (8 oz each) cream cheese, softened
- 1 cup sugar
- 1 tsp vanilla extract
- 3 eggs
- 1/2 cup sour cream

Instructions:

1. Preheat the oven to 325°F (163°C).
2. Combine graham cracker crumbs, sugar, and melted butter. Press the mixture into the bottom of a springform pan to form the crust. Bake for 10 minutes.
3. In a large bowl, beat the cream cheese, sugar, and vanilla extract until smooth.
4. Add the eggs, one at a time, mixing well after each addition.
5. Pour the batter into the prepared crust and bake for 50-60 minutes until the center is almost set.
6. Remove from the oven and let cool. Refrigerate for at least 4 hours before serving.
7. Top with fruit or chocolate sauce if desired.

Butter Chicken

Ingredients:

- 1 lb boneless chicken, cut into pieces
- 2 tbsp butter
- 1 onion, chopped
- 2 cloves garlic, minced
- 1 tbsp grated ginger
- 1/2 cup tomato puree
- 1/2 cup heavy cream
- 1 tbsp garam masala
- 1 tsp turmeric
- 1 tsp cumin
- 1/2 tsp chili powder
- Salt to taste

Instructions:

1. In a large pan, melt butter over medium heat. Add onions, garlic, and ginger. Cook until the onions are softened.
2. Add the tomato puree and spices (garam masala, turmeric, cumin, chili powder). Cook for 5 minutes until the sauce thickens.
3. Add the chicken pieces to the pan and cook until browned and cooked through, about 10-15 minutes.
4. Stir in the cream and cook for an additional 5 minutes.
5. Season with salt to taste and serve hot with rice or naan.

Milk-Based Smoothies

Ingredients:

- 1 cup milk (any variety)
- 1 banana
- 1/2 cup frozen berries (strawberries, blueberries, etc.)
- 1/2 cup yogurt
- 1 tsp honey or sweetener (optional)
- Ice cubes (optional)

Instructions:

1. Place all ingredients into a blender.
2. Blend until smooth and creamy.
3. Adjust sweetness by adding honey or sweetener if desired.
4. Serve immediately in a chilled glass.

Clotted Cream

Ingredients:

- 2 cups heavy cream (preferably non-ultra-pasteurized)
- 1/4 cup whole milk (optional for softer texture)

Instructions:

1. Pour the cream into a shallow dish and place it in the oven, preheated to 180°F (82°C).
2. Let the cream bake for 12 hours (overnight works well) without stirring. A golden crust will form on top.
3. After 12 hours, remove from the oven and cool at room temperature.
4. Once cooled, scrape off the thickened clotted cream from the top and transfer to a container.
5. Refrigerate and serve chilled on scones or with jam.

Chocolate Milk

Ingredients:

- 1 cup milk
- 2 tbsp cocoa powder
- 1-2 tbsp sugar (to taste)
- A pinch of salt
- 1/2 tsp vanilla extract (optional)

Instructions:

1. In a small saucepan, combine cocoa powder, sugar, and salt.
2. Add a small amount of milk and whisk until you form a smooth paste.
3. Gradually add the remaining milk and heat over medium heat, stirring until the chocolate is fully dissolved.
4. Remove from heat and stir in vanilla extract if desired.
5. Serve hot or cold, with ice cubes for a chilled version.

Milk Caramel Flan

Ingredients:

- 1 cup sugar (for caramel)
- 1 can sweetened condensed milk
- 1 can evaporated milk
- 3 large eggs
- 1 tsp vanilla extract
- A pinch of salt

Instructions:

1. Preheat the oven to 350°F (175°C).
2. To make the caramel: heat sugar in a saucepan over medium heat until it melts and turns amber. Pour the hot caramel into a flan mold or round baking dish.
3. In a blender, combine sweetened condensed milk, evaporated milk, eggs, vanilla, and salt. Blend until smooth.
4. Pour the custard mixture over the caramel in the baking dish.
5. Bake in a water bath for about 60-70 minutes, until set.
6. Let it cool completely before flipping it onto a plate to serve.

Dairy-Free Milk Alternatives (like Almond Milk)

Ingredients:

- 1 cup almonds (soaked overnight)
- 4 cups water
- 1 tsp vanilla extract (optional)
- Sweetener to taste (like honey, maple syrup, or stevia)

Instructions:

1. Drain and rinse the soaked almonds.
2. Blend the almonds with water in a high-speed blender until smooth.
3. Strain the mixture through a nut milk bag or fine mesh strainer to remove the almond pulp.
4. Transfer the almond milk to a clean jar and add vanilla extract and sweetener if desired.
5. Store in the refrigerator for up to 4 days. Shake before using.

Mascarpone Cheesecake

Ingredients:

- 1 1/2 cups graham cracker crumbs
- 1/4 cup sugar
- 1/2 cup melted butter
- 3 packages (8 oz each) mascarpone cheese
- 1 cup heavy cream
- 1 cup sugar
- 1 tsp vanilla extract
- 3 eggs

Instructions:

1. Preheat the oven to 325°F (163°C).
2. Combine graham cracker crumbs, sugar, and melted butter. Press into the bottom of a springform pan to form a crust.
3. Bake for 10 minutes, then set aside to cool.
4. In a large bowl, beat mascarpone cheese, sugar, and vanilla extract until smooth.
5. Add eggs, one at a time, and beat until well combined.
6. Pour the mixture over the crust and bake for 50-60 minutes, until set.
7. Let it cool completely, then refrigerate for at least 4 hours before serving.

Panna Cotta

Ingredients:

- 2 cups heavy cream
- 1 cup whole milk
- 1/2 cup sugar
- 1 tsp vanilla extract
- 2 1/2 tsp unflavored gelatin
- 3 tbsp cold water

Instructions:

1. In a small bowl, sprinkle the gelatin over cold water and let it bloom for 5 minutes.
2. In a saucepan, heat the cream, milk, and sugar over medium heat until sugar dissolves.
3. Remove from heat and stir in the gelatin until fully dissolved.
4. Stir in vanilla extract.
5. Pour the mixture into individual molds or cups and refrigerate for 4-6 hours or until set.
6. Serve with fresh berries or a fruit compote.

Rice and Milk Soup

Ingredients:

- 1/2 cup rice
- 4 cups milk
- 1/4 cup sugar
- 1 tsp cinnamon (optional)
- 1/4 tsp salt
- A dash of vanilla extract (optional)

Instructions:

1. Rinse the rice and add it to a large saucepan with the milk, sugar, cinnamon, and salt.
2. Bring to a simmer over medium heat, stirring occasionally.
3. Reduce the heat and let it cook for 20-25 minutes, stirring often, until the rice is tender and the mixture thickens.
4. Add vanilla extract if desired, and serve hot or chilled.

Milk-Based Ice Cream Sandwiches

Ingredients:

- 1 pint vanilla ice cream (or your favorite flavor)
- 1 package chocolate chip cookies (store-bought or homemade)

Instructions:

1. Scoop a small amount of ice cream onto the flat side of one cookie.
2. Place another cookie on top, pressing gently to form a sandwich.
3. Repeat with the remaining cookies and ice cream.
4. Freeze the sandwiches for at least 1 hour before serving, to firm up the ice cream.

Creamy Polenta

Ingredients:

- 1 cup polenta
- 4 cups milk (or a mix of milk and water)
- 2 tbsp butter
- 1/2 cup grated Parmesan cheese
- Salt and pepper to taste

Instructions:

1. In a medium saucepan, bring the milk (or milk-water mix) to a simmer.
2. Gradually whisk in the polenta, stirring constantly to prevent lumps.
3. Reduce the heat to low and continue cooking for about 20-25 minutes, stirring occasionally until the polenta is thick and tender.
4. Stir in the butter and Parmesan cheese.
5. Season with salt and pepper to taste, and serve hot as a side dish.

Milk Chocolate Cake

Ingredients:

- 1 3/4 cups all-purpose flour
- 1 1/2 cups sugar
- 1/2 cup cocoa powder
- 1 tsp baking powder
- 1/2 tsp baking soda
- 1/2 tsp salt
- 2 large eggs
- 1 cup milk
- 1/2 cup vegetable oil
- 1 tsp vanilla extract
- 1 cup boiling water

Instructions:

1. Preheat the oven to 350°F (175°C). Grease and flour a cake pan.
2. In a large bowl, mix the flour, sugar, cocoa powder, baking powder, baking soda, and salt.
3. Add the eggs, milk, vegetable oil, and vanilla extract. Mix until smooth.
4. Gradually pour in the boiling water and stir to combine. The batter will be thin.
5. Pour the batter into the prepared cake pan and bake for 30-35 minutes, or until a toothpick comes out clean.
6. Let the cake cool before serving or frosting.

Sweetened Condensed Milk Cookies

Ingredients:

- 1 cup all-purpose flour
- 1/2 cup sweetened condensed milk
- 1/4 cup butter (softened)
- 1/2 tsp vanilla extract
- 1/4 tsp baking powder
- A pinch of salt

Instructions:

1. Preheat the oven to 350°F (175°C) and line a baking sheet with parchment paper.
2. In a bowl, combine the flour, baking powder, and salt.
3. In another bowl, cream together the sweetened condensed milk, butter, and vanilla extract.
4. Gradually add the dry ingredients to the wet ingredients and mix until combined.
5. Drop spoonfuls of dough onto the prepared baking sheet, spacing them a few inches apart.
6. Bake for 10-12 minutes, until the edges are golden. Let cool before serving.

Milk-Custard Tart

Ingredients:

- 1 pre-baked tart shell
- 2 cups milk
- 1/2 cup sugar
- 1 tbsp cornstarch
- 2 large eggs
- 1 tsp vanilla extract

Instructions:

1. In a saucepan, heat the milk and sugar until warm, but not boiling.
2. In a bowl, whisk the eggs, cornstarch, and vanilla extract until smooth.
3. Gradually pour the warm milk into the egg mixture, whisking constantly to avoid curdling.
4. Return the mixture to the saucepan and cook over medium heat, stirring constantly until it thickens.
5. Pour the custard into the pre-baked tart shell and allow to cool before refrigerating for 2-3 hours.
6. Serve chilled with fresh fruit or whipped cream.

Milk Fudge (Kalakand)

Ingredients:

- 4 cups whole milk
- 1/2 cup sugar
- 1 tbsp lemon juice or vinegar
- 1/4 tsp cardamom powder
- Chopped pistachios (optional)

Instructions:

1. Heat the milk in a heavy-bottomed pan, stirring constantly, until it reduces by half.
2. Add the sugar and stir to dissolve.
3. Once the milk thickens, add the lemon juice or vinegar to curdle the milk and form paneer (cheese).
4. Continue cooking until the mixture thickens to a fudge-like consistency.
5. Stir in cardamom powder and transfer the mixture to a greased plate.
6. Let it cool and cut into squares. Garnish with chopped pistachios if desired.

Creamy Risotto

Ingredients:

- 1 1/2 cups Arborio rice
- 4 cups chicken or vegetable broth
- 1/2 cup dry white wine
- 1 cup milk
- 1/2 cup grated Parmesan cheese
- 1 small onion (chopped)
- 2 tbsp butter
- Salt and pepper to taste

Instructions:

1. In a saucepan, heat the broth and keep it warm.
2. In a large pan, melt the butter and sauté the chopped onion until soft.
3. Add the rice and stir to coat it with the butter.
4. Pour in the wine and cook until it's mostly absorbed.
5. Gradually add the warm broth, one ladleful at a time, stirring constantly until the liquid is absorbed before adding more.
6. After about 20-25 minutes, when the rice is tender, add the milk and Parmesan cheese.
7. Stir until the risotto is creamy and season with salt and pepper. Serve immediately.

Churned Butter

Ingredients:

- 2 cups heavy cream (preferably chilled)

Instructions:

1. Pour the cream into a stand mixer bowl or a jar with a tight-fitting lid.
2. Whisk or shake the cream for about 10-15 minutes until it thickens and the butter separates from the buttermilk.
3. Strain the butter from the buttermilk and rinse it under cold water.
4. Knead the butter with a spatula or in your hands to remove excess buttermilk.
5. Store the fresh butter in a container in the fridge.

Hot Chocolate

Ingredients:

- 2 cups milk
- 2 tbsp cocoa powder
- 2 tbsp sugar (or more to taste)
- 1/4 tsp vanilla extract
- Whipped cream or marshmallows (optional)

Instructions:

1. In a small saucepan, heat the milk over medium heat.
2. Whisk in the cocoa powder and sugar until fully dissolved.
3. Continue to heat until the mixture is hot but not boiling.
4. Stir in the vanilla extract and remove from heat.
5. Serve with whipped cream or marshmallows if desired.

Bechamel Sauce

Ingredients:

- 2 tbsp butter
- 2 tbsp all-purpose flour
- 2 cups milk
- Salt and pepper to taste
- 1/4 tsp nutmeg (optional)

Instructions:

1. In a saucepan, melt the butter over medium heat.
2. Whisk in the flour and cook for 1-2 minutes to form a roux.
3. Gradually add the milk while whisking constantly to avoid lumps.
4. Continue to cook, stirring, until the sauce thickens.
5. Season with salt, pepper, and nutmeg (if using). Use immediately.

Milk-Soaked French Toast

Ingredients:

- 4 slices bread
- 1 cup milk
- 2 large eggs
- 1 tsp cinnamon
- 1 tbsp sugar
- 1/2 tsp vanilla extract
- Butter for frying

Instructions:

1. In a shallow dish, whisk together the milk, eggs, cinnamon, sugar, and vanilla extract.
2. Heat a pan over medium heat and add a little butter.
3. Dip each slice of bread into the milk mixture, ensuring both sides are soaked.
4. Fry the bread in the pan until golden brown on both sides.
5. Serve with syrup, powdered sugar, or fruit.

Sweet Milk Buns

Ingredients:

- 2 cups all-purpose flour
- 1/2 cup warm milk
- 2 tbsp sugar
- 1 tbsp active dry yeast
- 1/4 cup melted butter
- 1/4 tsp salt
- 1 egg

Instructions:

1. In a bowl, dissolve the sugar in warm milk and add the yeast. Let it sit for 5-10 minutes to activate the yeast.
2. Add the flour, butter, salt, and egg to the yeast mixture. Mix to form a dough.
3. Knead the dough for about 5-7 minutes until smooth.
4. Cover and let the dough rise in a warm place for 1 hour or until doubled in size.
5. Preheat the oven to 350°F (175°C).
6. Punch down the dough and divide it into small balls. Place them on a greased baking sheet.
7. Bake for 15-20 minutes, until golden brown. Let them cool slightly before serving.

Milk Chocolate Truffles

Ingredients:

- 8 oz milk chocolate, chopped
- 1/2 cup heavy cream
- 1 tsp vanilla extract
- Cocoa powder, powdered sugar, or chopped nuts for rolling (optional)

Instructions:

1. Place the chopped milk chocolate in a heatproof bowl.
2. In a saucepan, heat the cream over medium heat until it begins to simmer.
3. Pour the hot cream over the chocolate and let it sit for a few minutes. Stir until smooth and combined.
4. Stir in the vanilla extract.
5. Refrigerate the mixture for about 2 hours or until firm enough to scoop.
6. Once firm, use a spoon or melon baller to shape the mixture into small balls.
7. Roll the truffles in cocoa powder, powdered sugar, or chopped nuts as desired.
8. Store in an airtight container in the refrigerator until ready to serve.

Hot Milk Cake

Ingredients:

- 1 cup milk
- 1/2 cup butter
- 1 1/2 cups all-purpose flour
- 1 cup sugar
- 2 tsp baking powder
- 1/4 tsp salt
- 2 large eggs
- 1 tsp vanilla extract

Instructions:

1. Preheat the oven to 350°F (175°C) and grease and flour an 8-inch round cake pan.
2. In a saucepan, heat the milk and butter over medium heat until the butter melts. Set aside.
3. In a bowl, whisk together the flour, sugar, baking powder, and salt.
4. In another bowl, beat the eggs and vanilla extract until smooth.
5. Gradually add the dry ingredients to the egg mixture, alternating with the warm milk and butter mixture.
6. Mix until well combined.
7. Pour the batter into the prepared cake pan and bake for 30-35 minutes or until a toothpick comes out clean.
8. Allow the cake to cool before serving.

Milk-Based Tiramisu

Ingredients:

- 1 1/2 cups milk
- 1 cup heavy cream
- 1/2 cup sugar
- 1 tsp vanilla extract
- 1 1/2 cups mascarpone cheese
- 1 package ladyfingers
- 1 cup strong brewed coffee, cooled
- 2 tbsp cocoa powder for dusting

Instructions:

1. In a saucepan, heat the milk, heavy cream, and sugar over medium heat until the sugar dissolves. Remove from heat and stir in the vanilla extract.
2. In a separate bowl, whisk the mascarpone cheese until smooth.
3. Gradually add the milk mixture to the mascarpone, stirring constantly until well combined.
4. Quickly dip the ladyfingers into the cooled coffee and layer them in the bottom of a dish.
5. Spread half of the mascarpone mixture over the ladyfingers and repeat with another layer of dipped ladyfingers.
6. Finish with the remaining mascarpone mixture and smooth the top.
7. Refrigerate for at least 4 hours, preferably overnight.
8. Before serving, dust with cocoa powder.

Strawberry Milk Pudding

Ingredients:

- 2 cups milk
- 1/4 cup sugar
- 2 tbsp cornstarch
- 1/2 tsp vanilla extract
- 1/2 cup fresh strawberries, pureed

Instructions:

1. In a saucepan, combine the milk, sugar, and cornstarch.
2. Heat the mixture over medium heat, stirring constantly until it thickens.
3. Remove from heat and stir in the vanilla extract.
4. Puree the strawberries in a blender or food processor, and add to the pudding mixture.
5. Pour the pudding into serving cups and refrigerate for at least 2 hours until set.
6. Serve chilled, garnished with fresh strawberry slices if desired.

Milk-Cream Cheese Frosting

Ingredients:

- 8 oz cream cheese, softened
- 1/4 cup butter, softened
- 1 1/2 cups powdered sugar
- 2 tbsp milk
- 1 tsp vanilla extract

Instructions:

1. In a bowl, beat the cream cheese and butter together until smooth and creamy.
2. Gradually add the powdered sugar, beating until combined.
3. Add the milk and vanilla extract, and continue beating until the frosting is smooth and fluffy.
4. Spread the frosting over cakes, cupcakes, or cookies. Store any leftovers in the refrigerator.

Homemade Ricotta

Ingredients:

- 4 cups whole milk
- 1 cup heavy cream
- 3 tbsp lemon juice or white vinegar
- 1/2 tsp salt

Instructions:

1. In a large saucepan, combine the milk and heavy cream and heat over medium heat until it reaches 190°F (88°C), stirring occasionally.
2. Remove from heat and add the lemon juice or vinegar, stirring gently. Let the mixture sit for 5 minutes as it curdles.
3. Line a fine-mesh strainer with cheesecloth and set it over a large bowl.
4. Pour the curdled milk mixture into the strainer, allowing the whey to drain off.
5. Let the ricotta drain for about 10-15 minutes, or longer for drier cheese.
6. Transfer the ricotta to a bowl and stir in the salt.
7. Use immediately or store in the refrigerator for up to 3 days.

Sweet Milk Yogurt Parfaits

Ingredients:

- 2 cups plain yogurt
- 1/4 cup sweetened condensed milk
- 1 tsp vanilla extract
- Fresh fruits (berries, mango, etc.)
- Granola or crushed nuts for topping

Instructions:

1. In a bowl, mix the yogurt, sweetened condensed milk, and vanilla extract until smooth and well combined.
2. Spoon a layer of the yogurt mixture into serving glasses.
3. Add a layer of fresh fruits on top of the yogurt.
4. Repeat the layers, finishing with a layer of yogurt.
5. Top with granola or crushed nuts for crunch.
6. Refrigerate for at least an hour before serving.

Caramelized Milk Pudding

Ingredients:

- 2 cups whole milk
- 1/2 cup sugar
- 1/4 cup cornstarch
- 1/2 tsp vanilla extract
- 1/4 tsp salt

Instructions:

1. In a saucepan, combine the milk and sugar over medium heat. Stir until the sugar is dissolved and the milk starts to simmer.
2. In a small bowl, mix the cornstarch with a little cold milk to form a slurry.
3. Slowly whisk the slurry into the simmering milk, and continue stirring until the mixture thickens.
4. Remove from heat and stir in the vanilla extract and salt.
5. Pour the pudding into serving dishes and let it cool to room temperature.
6. Refrigerate for at least 2 hours until set. Serve chilled.

Sweet Milk Tea

Ingredients:

- 2 cups water
- 2 black tea bags
- 1/4 cup sweetened condensed milk
- 1-2 tbsp sugar (optional)
- Ice cubes (optional)

Instructions:

1. Boil 2 cups of water in a saucepan.
2. Once the water is boiling, remove from heat and steep the tea bags for about 3-5 minutes.
3. Remove the tea bags and stir in the sweetened condensed milk and sugar, if using.
4. Let the tea cool to room temperature, or refrigerate it for a chilled version.
5. Serve over ice if desired.

Mashed Potatoes with Milk

Ingredients:

- 2 lbs potatoes, peeled and cut into chunks
- 1 cup whole milk
- 1/4 cup butter
- Salt and pepper to taste
- Chopped chives or parsley for garnish (optional)

Instructions:

1. In a large pot, boil the potatoes in salted water until tender, about 15-20 minutes.
2. Drain the potatoes and return them to the pot.
3. Add the butter and begin mashing.
4. Slowly add the milk, a little at a time, until the potatoes reach your desired consistency.
5. Season with salt and pepper to taste.
6. Garnish with chopped chives or parsley before serving.

Milk and Banana Smoothie

Ingredients:

- 1 ripe banana
- 1 cup whole milk
- 1 tbsp honey or maple syrup (optional)
- 1/2 tsp vanilla extract (optional)
- Ice cubes

Instructions:

1. Place the banana, milk, and optional honey or vanilla extract in a blender.
2. Add a few ice cubes and blend until smooth.
3. Pour into glasses and serve immediately.

Rice Milk Chocolate

Ingredients:

- 1/2 cup rice milk
- 1/2 cup dark or milk chocolate chips
- 2 tbsp coconut oil or butter
- 1/4 tsp vanilla extract
- Pinch of salt

Instructions:

1. In a saucepan, heat the rice milk over medium heat until it starts to simmer.
2. Remove from heat and stir in the chocolate chips, coconut oil, vanilla extract, and salt.
3. Stir until the chocolate is fully melted and smooth.
4. Pour the mixture into chocolate molds or a lined baking dish.
5. Refrigerate for at least 1-2 hours until the chocolate is firm.
6. Once set, remove from the molds and serve.